I0148715

Sylvester Sage Crosby

The United States Coinage of 1793, Cents and Half Cents

Descriptions of the various dies bearing that date with notes on the establishment

of the mint

Sylvester Sage Crosby

The United States Coinage of 1793, Cents and Half Cents
Descriptions of the various dies bearing that date with notes on the establishment of the mint

ISBN/EAN: 9783742862334

Manufactured in Europe, USA, Canada, Australia, Japa

Cover: Foto ©ninafisch / pixelio.de

Manufactured and distributed by brebook publishing software
(www.brebook.com)

Sylvester Sage Crosby

The United States Coinage of 1793, Cents and Half Cents

৵৵৵ THE CENTS OF 1793. ৵৵৵

By S. S. CROSBY.

Mr. CROSBY, well known to collectors of United States Cents, as one of the best if not highest authority on the " Early Coins of America," and especially the Colonial and first onal issues, has just published a Brochure in cap quarto size, of 36 pages and 3 photoures, on the Cents of 1793. The plates show accurate representations of ALL KNOWN eties of the Cents and Half Cents of that date, phototyped from original pieces, and some of the best known counterfeits. This will be an indispensable work to all colors of these pieces, as the descriptions are minute as to every detail.

ONLY A LIMITED EDITION has been printed.

Copies will be sent by mail on receipt of $2.00.

Address ED. FROSSARD,

108 E. 14th St., New York.

PLATE I
PATTERNS OF 1792 AND CENTS OF 1793.

HE UNITED STATES COINAGE OF 1793.--CENTS AND HALF CENTS.

DESCRIPTIONS OF THE VARIOUS DIES BEARING THAT DATE, WITH NOTES ON THE ESTABLISHMENT OF THE MINT.

By SYLVESTER SAGE CROSBY,

MEMBER OF THE BOSTON NUMISMATIC SOCIETY, HONORARY MEMBER OF THE AMERICAN NUMISMATIC AND ARCHAEOLOGICAL SOCIETY.

BOSTON:
PUBLISHED BY THE AUTHOR,
43 WEST STREET.
1897.

THE CENTS OF 1793.

THE discovery of new dies of the Cents of 1793, as well as of new combinations of dies previously known, has led me to undertake to describe them, trusting that with the assistance of collectors who have interested themselves in the study of the coinage of that year, I may be able to furnish descriptions of the whole of this interesting series.

That this confidence was justified is shown by the efforts of many to give me all possible aid, to all of whom my thanks are due, and especially to Dr. Thomas Hall, of Boston, whose cabinet lacks only one die (B) and one combination (14-K) of being complete, and which, as well as his more personal assistance has been ever at my service; to Mr. William S. Appleton, of Boston, Dr. Augustine Shurtleff, of Brookline, Mr. Edmund J. Cleveland, of Hartford, Conn., and Mr. R. Archer, Jr., of Dublin, Ireland, and others, who have kindly assisted me.

It is presumed that the illustrated article in the *American Journal of Numismatics*, of April, 1869, and more lately Mr. Frossard's Monograph, have directed the attention of collectors to this subject, and have instigated a search for new dies which should by this time have brought to light about all we can expect to find of the coinage of that year.

An additional incentive to the work was the fact that some of the dies which could not previously be minutely described, no well preserved specimens from them being then available, can now be clearly identified by means of pieces, which though not all entirely satisfactory, are much finer than could then be procured, and are probably the finest known specimens.

The descriptions may be thought to be too lengthy, and to enter too much into the minutiæ of the details; but it is designed to make them so definite that errors in identification may be avoided, and the recognition of every specimen be rendered certain even though much worn, or if no other impression from the die to which it is likened or with which it is compared, should be at hand for reference.

Mr. Ed. Frossard's valuable "Monograph," and the "Numismatic Study" of Mr. F. W. Doughty, are the only works beside the *Journal* already referred to, which have to my knowledge, especially illustrated this coinage. But I must differ from Mr. Frossard's estimate of the Cent he describes as No. 6, which is generally conceded to be from the same die with his No. 7 (see *Am. Journal of Numis.*, of Oct., 1888), but having, by a bruise, the stem of the left hand leaf thrown aside, apparently joining the stem of the centre leaf above the bruise, thus producing the appearance of a different sprig under the bust; and from Mr. Doughty in regard to the Cent originally described as the "Clover leaf Cent."

It is also intended to include the Half Cents of this year, and in this I think Mr. Frossard is alone, as I know of no other work making any attempt to illustrate and describe this portion of the coinage with any degree of completeness. The Washington pattern piece is all I am able to add to those he has given.

It was originally intended to confine this work to the coinage of 1793 alone, and not until the descriptions of the issues of that year were well advanced, in fact, nearly completed, did it occur to me to compare them with the patterns of 1792.

Upon making such comparisons, I was surprised that the similarity of some of the coins of 1793 to those patterns had not before been noticed.

Take for instance the "Birch" pattern Cent, the large pattern of 1792, shown as I on Plate 1. Omit the legend, except the word LIBERTY above the head, and place the date in exergue, which is, on the pattern, occupied by part of the legend, and we have with little variation the design of the obverse of the Cents of Class 2 of the issue of 1793. The design of the reverse is still more closely followed. The treatment of the hair in some of the dies of Class 2 also somewhat resembles that of the "Birch" pattern.

The head upon the small pattern Cent (II upon Plate 1), in some specimens struck with a plug of silver in the centre, to bring its intrinsic value to equal its face value (a degree of honesty long since abandoned, even in our silver coinage), is much unlike any other; apparently it is an Indian head, although in some respects it has a resemblance to those of Class 2 : but the reverse of this piece bears a close resemblance to reverse F, particularly in the formation of the bow.

In the pattern of the "Disme" (III) we have the nearest approach to the heads of Class 2, but facing the left, as does the head upon the Half Cents, instead of the right, as in the Cents.

There is one other pattern bearing the date of 1792 which is called a pattern Cent (IV), although it bears nothing to designate the value it was intended to represent. Its designs, both of obverse and reverse, more closely resemble some of the silver issues of the Mint, than any of its copper coins.

Mr. Wm. E. DuBois, then assayer at the U. S. Mint, wrote me, June, 1875, in reply to an inquiry regarding this pattern :—

The coin you refer to is in the Mint Cabinet, is of copper and weighs 175½ grains. Nothing is certainly known of its history; but as it was one of the pieces handed over to the Cabinet by the late Adam Eckfeldt, who was connected with the Mint from its origin,— and as it cannot well be referred to any other source, I feel pretty sure it is a trial piece, made in the Mint. I have never seen another. The lettering is feeble, but the devices are rather creditable. The edge is ribbed, like our present silver coin

The Half Disme (V), the head upon which much resembles that of the "Birch" Cent, has no especial bearing upon this subject, but is shown upon the Plate in order to complete this series of patterns. This is an extremely interesting piece, as it is said that Washington furnished a considerable amount of silver to be coined into " Half Dismes " for gifts to his friends.

Before entering upon my principal subject, it may be of interest to give the action taken by the authorities towards the establishment of a Mint, and the proceedings following that action, as well as some which preceded it.

An Act passed by Congress, April 2, 1792, ordained "That a Mint for the purpose of a national coinage be and the same is established ; to be situate and carried on at the seat of the government of the United States, for the time being."

Snowden in his " Mint Manual," says : —

Washington immediately proceeded to carry out the intention of this Act, and as Philadelphia was then the seat of government, he provided for the erection of suitable buildings, by purchasing a suitable lot of ground on Seventh street, between Market and Arch streets. * * * Washington, on the first of July following, appointed David Rittenhouse to be the "Director of the Mint." Rittenhouse very soon thereafter entered upon the duties of his office. * * * 1792, July 31. This day, about 10 o'clock in the forenoon, the foundation-stone was laid for the Mint, by David Rittenhouse, Esq. * * * The foundation was completed and ready for the superstructure on Saturday the 25th of August following, and the framework was raised in the afternoon of that day. The work was rapidly pushed forward after this date, and the building was so far completed that the workmen commenced operations "in the shop" preparing the internal arrangements, such as bellows, furnaces, etc., on Friday the seventh of September. On the Tuesday following, *six pounds of old copper* were purchased for the Mint, at " 1s 3d " per pound ; this being the first "purchase of copper for coining."

The coining presses (three in number) which they were obliged to import from abroad, arrived at the Mint on Friday, the 21st of September, and under date of 25th September * * * Flute began after breakfast, trimming the heavy press. These presses were put in operation in the beginning of October, and were used for striking the half dimes of which Washington makes mention in his Annual Address to Congress on the 6th of November, 1792, as follows : —

There has also been a small beginning in the coinage of half dimes ; the want of small coin in circulation calling the first attention to them. * * * The first *regular* return of coins from the chief coiner to the treasurer of the Mint took place on the 1st of March, 1793, and consisted of eleven thousand one hundred and seventy-eight cents.

John Harper, an extensive manufacturer of saws, at the corner of Sixth and Cherry streets, caused dies to be made under direction of Robert Birch. Most of the original Washington cent pieces were struck from these dies. The coins of 1791 were made in the cellar of Mr. Harper's shop, on a press which it is supposed was imported from England. The coins of 1792 were struck on a press which was set up in an old coach-house in Sixth-street, above Chestnut, directly opposite Jayne-street. This last described press was made by Adam Eckfeldt, for many years the chief coiner of the National Mint. (*Historical Magazine*, Vol. V, pp. 277-8.)

This account is confirmed by a letter received by me, 1874, from the late Jos. J. Mickley, of Philadelphia, who says a similar statement was made to him by Adam Eckfeldt, who was present and witnessed the coinage of some of those pieces.

The Cent was originally ordered to weigh 264 grains; the Half Cent in proportion; but on January 14, 1793, the weight of the Cent was reduced to 208 grains, and that of the Half Cent in the same ratio, to which weights the coins of that year closely approximate, the Cents ranging from 200 to 221 and the Half Cents from 100 to 106 grains. On January 26, 1796, Washington issued a proclamation stating that "on account of the increased price of copper, and the expense of coinage," the Cent should weigh but 7 dwts. or 168 grains, the Half Cent in proportion. This standard was retained until 1857, when the coinage of the large copper Cents and of the Half Cents was abandoned.

Several references are made by Thomas Jefferson, in his early writings, to the establishment of a mint and to engaging artists and machinery for prosecuting the work necessary in the coinage. The first was in a letter to Mr. Hopkinson, dated December 23d, 1786, in which he says: —

A person here has invented a method of coining the French Ecu of six livres, so as to strike both faces and the edge at one stroke, and makes a coin as beautiful as a medal. No country has ever yet produced such a coin. They are made cheaper, too: as yet he has only made a few to show the perfection of his manner. I am endeavoring to procure one to send to Congress as a model for their coinage. They will consider whether, on establishing a new mint, it will be worth while to buy his machines, if he will furnish them.

Mr. Jefferson evidently soon succeeded in procuring specimens of these pieces, for he writes to John Jay, under date of January 9, 1787 : —

Observing by the proceedings of Congress that they are about to establish a coinage, I think it my duty to inform them that a Swiss of the name of Drost, established here, has invented a method of striking the two faces and the edge of a coin at one stroke. By this and other simplifications of the process of coinage, he is enabled to coin from twenty-five thousand to thirty thousand pieces a day with the assistance of only two persons, the pieces of metal being first prepared. I send you by Colonel Franks, three coins of gold, silver and copper, which you will perceive to be perfect medals ; and I can assure you, from having seen him coin many, that every piece is as perfect as these. There has certainly never yet been seen any coin in any country comparable to this. The best workmen in this way, acknowledge that his is like a new art. Coin should always be made in the highest perfection possible, because it is a great guard against the danger of false coinage. This man would be willing to furnish his implements to Congress, and if they please, he will go over and instruct a person to carry on the work ; nor do I believe he would ask anything unreasonable. It would be very desirable, that in the institution of a new coinage, we could set out on so perfect a plan as this, and the more so, as while the work is so exquisitely done, it is done cheaper.

He writes to Mr. Grant from New York, April 23, 1790 : —

You may remember that we were together at the Hotel de la Monnoye to see Mr. Drost strike coins in his new manner, and that you were so kind as to speak with him afterwards on the subject of his coming to America. We are now in a condition to establish a Mint and should be desirous of engaging him in it. I suppose him to be at present in the service of Watts and Bolton, the latter of whom you may remember to have been present with us at the Monnoye. I know no means of communicating our dispositions to Drost so effectually as through your friendly agency, and therefore take the liberty of asking you to write to him, to know what emoluments he receives from Watts and Bolton, and whether he would be willing to come to us for the same ? If he will, you may give him an expectation, but without an absolute engagement, that we will call for him immediately, and that with himself, we may probably take and pay him for all the implements of coinage he may have, suited to our purpose. If he asks higher terms, he will naturally tell you so, and what they are, and we must reserve a right to consider of them. In either case, I will ask your answer as soon as possible. I need not observe to you that this negotiation should be known to nobody but yourself, Drost and Mr. Short.

The next letter upon this subject is to Mr. William Short, *Chargé d'Affaires* in France, written from Philadelphia, August 29, 1791 : —

You observe, that if Drost does not come, you have not been authorized to engage another coiner. If he does not come, there will probably be one engaged here. If he comes, I should think him a safe hand to send the diplomatic dye by, as also all the dyes of our medals, which may be used here for striking off what shall be wanting hereafter. But I would not have them trusted at sea, but from April to October, inclusive. Should you not send them by Drost, Havre will be the best route. I have not spoken with the Secretary of the Treasury yet, on the subject of the presses, but believe you may safely consider two presses as sufficient for us, and agree for no more without a further request.

And again he writes to the same, under date of November 24, 1791 : —

You mention that Drost wishes the devices of our money to be sent to him, that he may engrave them there. This cannot be done, because not yet decided on. The devices will be fixed by the law which shall establish the Mint.

He writes to Mr. Pinckney, from Philadelphia, June 14, 1792 : —

The United States being now about to establish a Mint, it becomes necessary to ask your assistance in procuring persons to carry on some parts of it ; and to enable you to give it, you must be apprized of some facts.

Congress, some time ago, authorized the President to take measures for procuring some artists from any place where they were to be had. It was known that a Mr. Drost, a Swiss, had made an improvement in the method of coining, and some specimens of his coinage were exhibited here, which were superior to anything we had ever seen. Mr. Short was, therefore, authorized to engage Drost to come over to erect the proper machinery and instruct persons to go on with the coinage ; and, as he supposed this would require about a year, we agreed to give him a thousand Louis a year and his expenses. The agreement was made, two coining mills (or screws) were ordered by him, but in the end, he declined coming. We have reason to believe he was drawn off by the English East India Company, and that he is now at work for them in England. Mr. Bolton had also made a proposition to coin for us in England, which was declined. Since this, the act has been passed for establishing our mint, which authorizes among other things, the employment of an assayer at fifteen hundred dollars a year, a chief coiner at the same, and an engraver at twelve hundred dollars. But it admits of the employment of one person, both as engraver and chief coiner; this we expect may be done, as we presume that any engraver who has been used to work for a coinage, must be well enough acquainted with all the operations of coinage to direct them; and it is an economy worth attention, if we can have the services performed by one officer instead of two, in which case, it is proposed to give him the salary of the chief coiner (that is to say), fifteen hundred dollars a year. I have therefore, to request, that you will endeavor on your arrival in Europe, to engage and send us an assayer of approved skill and well-attested integrity, and a chief coiner and engraver, in one person, if possible, acquainted with all the improvements in coining, and particularly those of Drost and Bolton. Their salaries may commence from the day of their sailing for America. If Drost be in England, I think he will feel himself under some obligation to aid you in procuring persons. How far Bolton will do it, seems uncertain. You will, doubtless, make what you can of the good dispositions of either of these or any other person. Should you find it impracticable to procure an engraver capable of performing the functions of chief coiner also, we must be content that you engage separate characters. Let these persons bring with them all the implements necessary for carrying on the business, except such as you shall think too bulky and easily made here. It would be proper, therefore, that they should consult you as to the necessary implements and their prices, that they may act under your control. The method of your paying for these implements and making reasonable advances to the workmen, shall be the subject of another letter, after the President shall have decided thereon. It should be a part of the agreement of these people, that they will faithfully instruct all persons in their art, whom we shall put under them for that purpose. Your contract with them may be made for any term not exceeding four years.

P.S. Should you not be able to procure persons of eminent qualifications for their business in England, it will be proper to open a correspondence with Mr. Morris on the subject, and see whether he cannot get such from France. Next to the obtaining the ablest artists, a very important circumstance is to send them to us as soon as possible.

The last we hear of these negotiations is in a letter dated April 20, 1793, which he writes to Mr. Pinckney : —

We shall be glad to receive the assayer you hope to procure, as soon as possible, for we cannot get one in this country equal to the business in all its parts. With respect to Mr. Drost, we retain the same desire to engage him, but we are forced to require an immediate decision, as the officer employed in the interim, and who does tolerably well, will not continue much longer under an uncertainty of permanent employment. I must therefore, desire you to press Mr. Morris to bring Drost to an immediate determination ; and we place the matter on this ground with him, that, if he is not embarked by the first day of July next, we shall give a permanent commission to the present officer, and be free to receive no other. We are likely to be in very great distress for copper for the mint, and must therefore press your expediting what we desired you to order from Sweden.

For the copper here referred to, a letter of March 16, 1793, states : —

I now enclose you the Treasurer's record of exchange for twenty-four thousand seven hundred and fifty guilders, to be employed for the purchase of copper for the mint, from Sweden, or wherever else it can be got on the best terms, the first of exchange having been enclosed in my letter of December the 30th.

To go back a little in time, I will here introduce a proposition received by the Government from Mr. John H. Mitchell, of England, for furnishing a supply of coins, April 15, 1790 : —

The Secretary of State, to whom was referred, by the House of Representatives, the letter of John H. Mitchell, reciting certain proposals for supplying the United States with copper coinage, has had the same under consideration, according to instructions, and begs leave to report thereon as follows : —

The person who wishes to undertake the supply of a copper coinage, sets forth, that the superiority of his apparatus and process for coining, enables him to furnish a coinage better and cheaper than can be done by any country or person whatever ; that his dies are engraved by the first artist in that line in Europe ; that his apparatus for striking the edge at the same blow with the faces, is new, and singularly ingenious : that he coins on a press on a new principle, and worked by a fine engine, more regularly than can be done by hand; that he will deliver any quantity of coin, of any size and device, of pure, unalloyed copper, wrapped in paper and packed in casks, ready for shipping, for fourteen pence sterling, the pound.

The Secretary of State has before been apprised, from other sources of information, of the great improvements made by this undertaker, in sundry arts; he is acquainted with the artist who invented the method of striking the edge and both faces of the coin at one blow; he has seen his process and coins, and sent to the former Congress some specimens of them, with certain offers from him, before he entered into the service of the present undertaker (which specimens he takes the liberty of now submitting to the inspection of the House, as proofs of the superiority of this method of coinage, in gold and silver as well as copper).

He is, therefore, of opinion, that the undertaker, aided by that artist, and by his own excellent machines, is truly in a condition to furnish coins in a state of higher perfection than has ever yet been issued by any nation; that perfection in the engraving is among the greatest safeguards against counterfeits, because engravers of the first class are few, and elevated by their rank in their art, far above the base and dangerous business of counterfeiting. That the perfection of coins will indeed disappear, after they are for some time worn among other pieces, and, especially where the figures are rather faintly relieved, as on those of this artist; yet, their high finishing, while new, is not the less a guard against counterfeits, because these, if carried to any extent, may be ushered into circulation new, also, and consequently, may be compared with genuine coins in the same state; that, therefore, whenever the United States shall be disposed to have a coin of their own, it will be desirable to aim at this kind of perfection. That this cannot be better effected, than by availing themselves, if possible, of the services of the undertaker, and of this artist, whose excellent methods and machines are said to have abridged, as well as perfected, the operations of coinage. These operations, however, and their expense, being new, and unknown here, he is unable to say whether the price proposed be reasonable or not. He is also uncertain, whether, instead of the larger copper coin, the Legislature might not prefer a lighter one of billon, or mixed metal, as is practiced, with convenience, by several other nations — a specimen of which kind of coinage is submitted to their inspection.

But, the propositions under consideration suppose that the work is to be carried on in a foreign country, and that the implements are to remain the property of the undertaker; which conditions, in his opinion render them inadmissable, for these reasons :

13

Coinage is peculiarly an attribute of sovereignty. To transfer its exercise into another country, is to submit it to another sovereign.

Its transportation across the ocean, besides the ordinary dangers of the sea, would expose it to acts of piracy, by the crews to whom it would be confided, as well as by others apprised of its passage.

In time of war, it would offer to the enterprises of an enemy, what have been emphatically called the sinews of war.

If the war were with the nation within whose territory the coinage is, the first act of war, or reprisal, might be to arrest this operation, with the implements and materials coined and uncoined, to be used at their discretion.

The reputation and principles of the present undertaker are safeguards against the abuses of a coinage, carried on in a foreign country, where no checks could be provided by the proper sovereign, no regulations established, no police, no guard exercised; in short, none of the numerous cautions hitherto thought essential at every mint; but in hands less entitled to confidence, these will become dangers. We may be secured, indeed, by proper experiments as to the purity of the coin delivered us according to contract, but we cannot be secured against that which, though less pure, shall be struck in the genuine die, and protected against the vigilance of Government till it shall have entered into circulation.

We lose the opportunity of calling in and re-coining the clipped money in circulation, or we double our risk by a double transportation.

We lose, in like manner, the resource of coining up our household plate in the instant of great distress.

We lose the means of forming artists to continue the works; when the common accidents of mortality shall have deprived us of those who began them.

In fine, the carrying on a coinage in a foreign country, as far as the Secretary knows, is without example; and general example is weighty authority.

He is, therefore, of opinion, on the whole, that a Mint, whenever established, should be established at home; that the superiority, the merit, and means of the undertaker, will suggest him as the proper person to be engaged in the establishment and conduct of a Mint, on a scale which, relinquishing nothing in the perfection of the coin, shall be duly proportioned to our purposes.

And, in the meanwhile, he is of opinion the present proposals should be declined.

April 14th, 1790.   THOMAS JEFFERSON.

I have tried to ascertain by whom the dies for the Cents of 1793 were cut, but I find no more definite information than that furnished by the action of our agents, already quoted, and that given by Mr. Patterson DuBois, of the United States Mint, in the *American Journal of Numismatics* for July, 1883.

Judging from the first of these sources, the dies for Class 1 may have been cut by Jean Pierre Droz.¹ The faint relief of these coins certainly agrees with the description given above of Mitchell's specimens, and from his evident connection with Droz and his reference to the Secretary's knowledge of the methods invented by that engraver, who is shown by the letter to have been in Mitchell's service, it is clear that he is the person styled "the first artist in Europe" and the engraver of the specimens sent by Mr. Mitchell. For these reasons I am inclined to attribute to him the dies alluded to, viz.: Class 1. The later negotiation of our agents with Droz himself, together with the similarity in the style of workmanship of the earliest Cents to Mitchell's specimens, submitted in 1790, as described, render it probable that the dies of these Cents were the work of the same artist, especially as reference is found to him alone, in this line, and as the negotiations with him must have continued until after our coinage had actually begun, the latest reference to them being April 20, 1793, and the coins being put into circulation March 1, of that year.

Quoting from Mr. DuBois's letter, before referred to: "Robert Scot received his appointment as the first Engraver of the Mint, November 23, 1793. According to Loubat, Joseph Wright 'was appointed first draughtsman and die-sinker to the United States Mint.' . . . Wright died in 1793. The Mint did not fairly get into operation until October, 1794, though there was some coinage before that, as is generally known. 'Struck off a few pieces of copper coin,' says an old expense book, the entry dated December 17, 1792; — probably the first. Wright must have made some of these earliest dies,

1 Droz, whose name is frequently spelled Drost in the official correspondence, is undoubtedly Jean Pierre Droz, a Swiss engraver of coin and medal dies. He was born in 1746, and settled in Paris in 1766. He was for a time in England, as appears in the text, but subsequently returned to France, and was a prominent engraver of public medals and coins during the Empire. He died in 1823.

but Robert Scot is the first officer of the line." It thus appears probable that J. P. Droz cut the dies for Class 1. Joseph Wright, those of Class 2, and Robert Scot, those of Class 3.

In order to prove the priority of the Cents having the chain upon the reverse, and to show the criticism which they provoked, I quote (with a slight correction) a paragraph from a Philadelphia paper of March 18, 1793 : —

> The American Cents (says a letter from Newark) do not answer our expectation. The chain on the reverse is but a bad omen for liberty, and liberty herself appears to be in a fright. May she not justly cry out in the words of the Apostle, " Alexander the copper-smith did me much evil: the Lord reward him according to his works!"

The Cents of 1793 may be arranged in three classes, the heads upon all facing to the right, as follows : —

Class 1.   The *Chain or Link* Cents, having on their reverses a chain of fifteen links.   Of these, I find four obverse and three reverse dies.

Class 2.   The *Wreath* Cents, having on their reverses a wreath, the stems of which are tied with a single bow-knot.   Seven obverses and six reverses are found here.

Class 3.   The *Liberty-Cap* Cents, taking their name from the design of the obverse, but having upon the reverse a wreath tied with a double bow-knot.   Of this class, I have found but three obverses and two reverses.

CLASS 1.   THE CHAIN OR LINK CENTS.

This class comprises obverses 1, 2, 3 and 4, with reverses A, B and C. The heads are "faintly relieved," as the samples furnished by Mitchell were described to have been, and have the hair in fine locks, being very much alike in all the dies. The legend, LIBERTY, is above the head, and the date, 1793, in exergue. The reverses have the words ONE CENT and the fraction 1/100 within an endless chain of fifteen links, which is encircled by the legend, UNITED STATES OF AMERI. (or AMERICA)   Around the field of both obverse and reverse is a slightly raised or milled rim.   The edges are divided into four unequal sections, the two smaller of which are lightly reeded, the two larger being filled by a vine (?), or by a series of sprays resembling a vine, bearing small trefoil or trilobed leaves, and blossoms, or, more probably cotton leaves and bolls of cotton. This edge was formerly known as "stars and stripes," but is now usually, and more correctly, called "vine and bars." The sizes vary from twenty-five to twenty-eight millimetres, and the weights from two hundred to two hundred and twenty-one grains.

Obverse 1, with reverses A and C. A head of Liberty, facing the right, with hair in fine locks flowing backward and downward, the lower locks long and slender. The letters of the legend — LIBERTY — are regular in size and spacing, and equally distant from the rim and the head. The figures of the date are widely spaced, being separated nearly two millimetres, the space between 7 and 9 fully of that extent. The point of the bust is short and curved, terminating in a sharp point two and one-half millimetres from the top of the figure 3. A short lock of hair just below the angle formed by the hair and the neck-line of the bust, points downward between the 7 and 9. The two longer thin locks at the left extend about as far as the inner circle of the date, the third lock being still longer.

Reverse A, with obverse 1. An endless chain of fifteen links, enclosing the words ONE CENT and the fraction $\frac{1}{100}$. A small point, the centre-mark of the die, appears between the tops of E and N of CENT, and both words are equally distant from the chain on either side. The legend is UNITED STATES OF AMERI. The period is small and about its own diameter distant from the I. The line or rule of division in the fraction (regula) is nearly two millimetres below the word CENT and equally distant from the numerator and the ciphers of the denominator, but very near the figure 1 of the latter. The space between 1 and 00 is wide. C of CENT and U of UNITED low, F of OF high.

Obverse 2, with reverse C. The legend is regularly, but widely spaced, and nearly twice as far from the rim as from the head. The hair is longer, flowing down closely at the left of the date, the longest locks at the extreme left reaching nearly as far as its outer circle ; five of the lower locks are long, and a small lock in the angle of the neck points toward the 3. One fine lock strays down nearly to the top of the 1, and a slight crack from the border crosses that figure. The date is more closely spaced than on obverse 1, and I will here note that the spaces of the date show a gradual decrease from obverse 1 to obverse 4. This is most noticeable between the 9 and 3, but nearly as much so between 7 and 9, excepting between the figures on obverses 2 and 3, which are more nearly equal. Only one from this die known.

Obverse 3, with reverses B and C. The letters of the legend irregular in size and position, and near the head, as in obverse 1. The R, large, high and leaning to right. Seven lower locks of hair long and farther to the left of the date than in obverses 1 and 2. The short lock nearest the angle of the neck-line points at the figure 1. The line of the neck is nearly straight and the point of the bust narrow and straight. The date is nearer to the point of the bust than to the hair, and the 7, low. The form or outline of the chain upon the reverse is often found incused on this obverse in front of the mouth and throat, and under the neck, probably caused by a partial impression of the reverse die being received by the obverse from an accidental contact without an intervening planchet.

Reverse B, with obverse 3. The legend is UNITED STATES OF AMERI. CENT is very near the chain on the right. No centre-mark. The first s of STATES is low; 1, of UNITED, F, and MER, high. The period following the legend is large, and more than twice its own diameter from the letter 1. The regula high; the figures smaller than those of reverse A, and the numerator rests on the line. 100 evenly spaced, but the ciphers low. I have found only one impression of this die and cannot now trace that, but describe and illustrate it from a copy taken some years ago.

Obverse 4, with reverse C. The letters of the legend are more closely spaced, and nearer the rim than the head. L and D are low, L and 1 very close. Many of the lower locks are long, some reaching nearly as far as the outer circle of the date. The date closely spaced and both legend and date are followed by a period.

Reverse C, with obverses 1, 2, 3 and 4. This die bears a close resemblance to reverse B, differing only in the legend, which in this is UNITED

STATES OF AMERICA, the C and A low. All peculiarities noted in B are found also in this, and I conclude that the same hub was used in sinking the die, but altered by the obliteration of the period, and by the addition of CA to the legend: and these letters, when added, were placed lower than the others. A detailed description would be a mere repetition of that already given for reverse B, except in the particulars noted above.

The Cents of Class 1 may be estimated in their order of rarity as: —

First, 2-C and 3-B.

Second, 1-A and 4-C.

Third, 1-C and 2-C.

CLASS 2. THE WREATH CENTS.

This class includes obverses 5 to 11, with reverses D to J inclusive. These have been known as the "Wreath Cents," but they might be more definitely designated as the Single-bow Wreath Cents, for the Liberty Cap Cents also have wreaths upon their reverses, but the stems are tied with a double bow knot.

The heads are in bolder relief than the preceding, which gives them a larger and heavier appearance. A double curl of hair is in the angle between the lower locks and the neck-line of the bust. The hair flows more loosely, in longer, heavier and more separate tresses, closely resembling the French ideal head of Liberty, but without the cap and staff. Above the head (which in the several dies differs but slightly, and chiefly in the treatment of the hair) is the legend, LIBERTY Under the bust, and above the date 1793 which is in exergue, is a sprig of three leaves. Near the edge is a circle of fine beads or pellets, forming the border.

The reverses have the words ONE CENT within a wreath formed by two curved branches bearing leaves, most of which are ovate, a few being trefoils, among which are numerous axillary racemes of fruit or berries (?). In every die a single trefoil is found upon the inside of each branch, and upon only one is the branch without one or more upon the outside. The stems of the branches are crossed below, and tied with a ribbon which forms within the wreath a single bow, the ends falling below the stems, leaving an intervening space which is occupied by the fraction $\frac{1}{100}$. The legend UNITED STATES OF AMERICA nearly encircles the wreath. Near the edge is a beaded border, as on the obverse.

Before describing these dies, some remarks concerning the first of their obverses, as well as all the reverses of Classes 2 and 3 may not be amiss. There has been much difference of opinion regarding the Cent with obverse 5. The term "Clover leaf" was applied to it when it was, I think, first brought into general notice in the *American Journal of Numismatics*, in April, 1869; I cannot now say by whom this name was originated, and it has since been called the "Strawberry leaf," and more recently the "Laurel-blossom" Cent.

Neither of these terms seeming to exactly suit the case, I have endeavored to ascertain the real design of the artist in placing upon this die a sprig so different from that on any other of these coins, and I am now convinced that he intended to represent a sprig of three leaves and a boll of cotton. The leaf does not indeed exactly represent the form of most of the leaves of the cotton plant, but among them are found some tri-lobed leaves similar to those here shown : and when I requested an artist to draw for me a cotton leaf, he sketched one closely resembling those of this sprig and the trefoil, or rather tri-lobed leaves of the wreaths upon the reverses of the Cents of this class, which are identically the same as the leaves of this sprig. An examination of the cotton leaves upon the reverses of the " Flying eagle " Cents of 1857 and 1858, and the Dimes and Five-cent nickel coins of 1883 and later, will show the forms in which the cotton leaf is represented, some of them differing no more from the leaves of this sprig than from each other, but they show the latitude displayed by artists in conventionalizing their subjects.

The wreaths upon the reverses have by some been called laurel, and by others, olive. They do not accurately represent either, but more closely resemble the olive, as in that the fruit is borne upon racemes springing from the axils of the leaves, but usually singly, rather than in clusters, while the berries of the laurel are borne in umbels at the ends of the branches. The axillary racemes in slender sprays, as here shown, are found on neither laurel nor olive ; but the American olive has axillary racemes of blossoms and fruit, which would require but little change to render them like these when drawn on as small a scale ; upon the reverses of the Liberty-cap Cents, the intention to represent the olive is evident. In describing the leaves of the wreath, I shall however, adhere to the former terms of ovate and trefoil (some of them are elliptical and lanceolate, others tri-lobed) which, if not botanically correct, will be well understood, and have usually been used in similar descriptions.

It is interesting to note that on some of the most ancient of the Greek coins, notably those of Arcadia with the head of Hera, there is a sprig of three olive leaves in the space below the chin of the goddess, which is strikingly suggestive of the similar sprig on our first Cent, and it may give an additional interest to these pieces if we mention that the helmet of the goddess Athene, as shown on the Athenian coins, was crowned with a wreath of olive, her sacred plant, after the battle of Marathon which did so much to establish the freedom of Greece ; and the helmet bore this wreath for more than two centuries, or until the head of the statue by Phidias which stood in the Parthenon was substituted for the earlier type,[1] at which time the olive wreath, enlarged and formed of two stems bearing leaves and berries, tied or bound at the base and open at the top, was placed on the reverse. This, I believe, is one of the earliest instances of the use of a wreath as a type on Greek coins.[2] Whether these devices suggested the design on the dies for our early Cents, or have any bearing on the question whether the wreath on those Cents is olive or laurel, I shall not discuss at length. But it is a singular coincidence, to say the least, to find the spray of olive leaves and the wreath of two olive branches on the first issues of our National Mint and upon these ancient Greek coins.

---

[1] See *Journal* for January, 1896, pp. 72 and 74.

[2] There are several coins of Delphos which bear laurel wreaths, struck in the fourth century, B. C.

PLATE II.
THE CENTS OF 1793.
Band at foot shows edge device.

It must be admitted that this device is more artistic than the chain, which was ridiculed at once as incongruous with Liberty, but which was doubtless adopted as symbolizing the Union, and which had been used on the Fugios of 1787; and since the work of Droz on French medals bearing the head of Louis XVI, and on others struck under Napoleon, shows him to have been possessed of superior ability, whether or not he was "the first artist in Europe," as claimed by Mitchell, may it not be possible, as the collections of ancient coins were more readily accessible to him than to American engravers, that he suggested, if he did not design the devices for the Cents of Class 2, (the olive sprig beneath the head and the wreath), drawing his inspiration from the old Greek coins?

As further tending to show that the wreath was originally intended to represent olive, and not laurel, it is to be observed that the wreath on the second issue of the Dollar of 1795 represents in the branch on the left the olive, which resembles the branches on the reverse of the Liberty-cap Cents, while that on the right has more elongated, narrow and sharply pointed leaves and no berries, evidently designed to represent a branch of palm.

Obverse 5, with reverses D and E. This is the obverse already referred to as having been first known as the "Clover leaf" Cent, but which I think may properly be called the Cotton leaf Cent, and is the greatest rarity of its class, only three specimens being known to collectors, one having reverse D, and two, reverse E. It bears upon a stem rising from near the angle of the 7, three trefoil leaves and a blossom, or boll of cotton. The legend and date are in small characters, the R larger and higher than the other letters and placed over the hair, close above the forehead. The date is less than two millimeters from the hair at the left, and more than four from the point of the bust, which is longer and more rounded at its tip than in any other known die. The double curl under the neck is rather heavy. It is difficult to account for the scarcity of specimens from this die, as it appears to have been thought worthy of two reverse dies, neither it, or either of its reverses showing any signs of deterioration, and neither reverse being known to have been used with any other obverse. It is hoped that better specimens of these may yet be discovered.

Reverse D, with obverse 5. $\frac{ONE}{CENT}$ central in the wreath, the centre-mark under N and equally distant from each word: C of CENT low, and T high. The branch at the left bears fifteen ovate and two trefoil leaves; that at the right, fourteen ovate and two trefoils: on the left, both trefoils are half below the lower line of CENT, those on the right mostly below: the upper terminal leaves are all single, that at the right pointing between two at the left. The left branch has eight sprays of berries outside and two inside; the right, six (?) outside and five inside; the upper spray at the left is of four (?) berries starting from the point of the second outer leaf, and apparently pointing toward OF. The stems below the knot are of about equal length, that at the left close to the ribbon near its end; that at the right, in contact with a curve of the ribbon end for more than half its length, and both terminate near the ends of the legend. The ribbon is heavy and forked at its ends, and the bow low, broad, and depressed at its top. The fraction is high, and central in the space between the ribbon ends: the regula is short, slightly curved, heavy at its ends, and close under the numerator. Only one impression is known from this die.

Reverse E, with obverse 5. $\frac{ONE}{CENT}$ high, the centre-mark in the middle of CENT, NT low. The left branch bears seventeen ovate leaves and but one trefoil; the right, fifteen ovate and two trefoils: all the trefoils are on line with the top of the bow: the upper terminal leaf at the left is single, the upper spray of three berries starting from its side and pointing close to the right of S: the right branch has a double terminal, pointing between two leaves at the left; the left branch has six sprays of berries outside and three inside; the right, six outside and only one on the inside. The bow is more nearly heart-shaped, the ribbon lighter, its ends less forked and shorter, not reaching, on the left, to the inner circle of the legend,[1] and farther from it there than on the right. The fraction is low and a little to the right, the regula slightly curved, high, reaching under the ribbon end at the right.

[1] Outer or inner circle of the legend, indicates a circle which would just enclose or be enclosed by the legend.

This is the only die having a branch with no trefoil upon the outside. Only two impressions from it are known.

Obverse 6, with reverse F. The head is in bold relief with hair in heavy locks. The letters of the legend are large, nearly filling the space between the head and the border: the date also large, widely spaced and rather nearer the point of the bust than to the hair: R is over the hair close above the forehead. The lower lock of hair is heavy, and forked or double at its end, the longer point reaching nearly to the border; the two next above it finer and distinctly separated, leaving the field between them clear; the double curl under the neck not very heavy. Under the bust on this and of all of this class which follow, is a sprig of three ovate leaves: the stem of this sprig rises from near the angle of the 7; the leaves are large; the two lower rise slightly from the horizontal, the central leaf leaning a little to the right. This is quite a scarce die.

Reverse F, with obverses 6, 7, 8 and 10. ONE CENT high, the centre-mark in the middle of CENT. The left branch bears nineteen ovate and three trefoil leaves; the right, fifteen ovate and three trefoil: two trefoils on each branch are on the outside, those at the left under N and D, that on the inside under C; the three on the right are closely grouped under IC of the legend: the left branch has six sprays of berries outside, and four inside; the right, seven outside and four inside: the upper spray on the left is of four berries, starting from the side of the first leaf and points midway between S and O; the terminal leaf at the left points between two at the right. The bow is smaller and heavier than that of any other of these dies: the ribbon is very heavy, and in forming the bow is folded backward, the edge showing within the loop, greatly contracting the space within it: the ribbon ends are broad and heavy, reaching nearly to the border: the stem at the left lies very close to the ribbon for nearly its whole length, that at the right is clear of the ribbon and nearly touches the foot of A. The fraction is low and central: the regula straight and low, reaching nearly across the space. The legend is very near the border. This is the only die having three trefoils on each branch.

After these reverses were arranged it was noticed that there was a gradual decrease in the distance between the border and the legend, from F to J;
and the size of the leaves of the sprig upon the obverse shows nearly as con-
stant and regular a decrease between obverses 6 and 11, coupled with them.

Obverse 7, with reverse F. The head is much like that of No. 6, but
the hair more massive, and in heavier tresses, the lower lock double as in
that, but heavier and longer, nearly reaching the border: the double curl
under the neck is heavy, the legend and date much smaller; the letters irregular in size and position, 1 high and leaning to left, R large and Y over the
line of separation between the hair and the forehead: the date is less than
one millimeter from the hair, and about five from the point of the bust: the
7 is small and lightly cut: the stem of the sprig, the leaves of which are
large, as in No. 6, but not as widely spread, rises from midway over 7 and 9,
curving upward to the right, the leaf at that side lying horizontally over 3,
and reaching beyond it: the leaf at the left lies closely up between the lower
lock and the double curl, but that at the right is three millimeters from the
point of the bust. This is nearly as scarce as obverse 6. The coins from
this die are usually slightly convex, as it probably " caved " or yielded across
the centre, — a line or slight crack showing on some specimens, from the
border to the mouth, and the die giving way more across and behind the head.
It is known as the warped or sprung die.

Obverse 8, with reverse F. The head is not as massive as those of Nos.
6 and 7. The locks of hair are cleanly and singly cut, and distinctly separate
as in No. 6: the lower tresses are not as heavy, and the second is nearer to
the first (the lowest) than to the third, the lowest two parallel, nearly reaching the border: all the hair is in finer and more separate locks: T is over the
hair, close above the forehead: the double curl is very light, and formed by
a single loop with a small lock hanging from it and joining the tip of the leaf
at the left of the sprig. The letters of the legend are slightly smaller and
lighter than those of obverse 7, more regular in size and more widely spaced.
The date is widely spaced, 79 and 3 very close to the border. The stem of
the sprig starts from just above the left of 9, curving slightly to the right:

the leaf at the left is wider than the centre leaf, that at the right, narrower, being not more than half the size of that at the left.

The discovery of this obverse was a curious instance of the appearance of a new die after a search of many years over a large field. Nearly ten years after the publication of the article on these Cents in the *Journal of Numismatics*, in 1869, when we had most of the important collections at our service, and a thorough search had been made in all directions, a lot of about seventy-five worn-out 1793 Cents was sent me from Philadelphia, for examination. Among these I found two pieces from a die hitherto unnoticed, the only feature sufficiently preserved to distinguish them being the sprig under the bust. I learned of no similar piece for another ten years, when a better specimen was shown me, belonging to Mr. Henry Phelps, of Worcester, Mass.; but in the Winsor sale of 1895, a fine and well-preserved specimen was discovered and purchased by its present owner, Dr. Thomas Hall, of Boston, and was by him alone recognized as from this rare die. This is the piece represented upon the plate. The two worn pieces first found are still in my possession, but are in so poor condition that they should not be considered as affecting its rarity, which should be estimated as only short of unique.[1]

Obverse 9, with reverses G, H, and I.[2] The head is much like that of obverse 7, the hair being full and the tresses nearly as heavy as on that, but not as full and long behind the head; the three lower locks are of about equal length, all almost reaching the border, and nearly parallel to each other, the second nearer to the third than to the first; the double curl joins the tip of the leaf at the left of sprig. The letters of the legend are much like those of obverse 8, but more closely spaced. L is low, Y high, and 7 large and high. The distinctive feature of this is the sprig, which is of three narrow leaves, the two at the right on a separate stem which, as well as that

1 The *American Journal of Numismatics* observes that this is known as the "Crosby Cent," from the fact that the writer first discovered and pointed out the die-differences mentioned in the text.

2 In Mr. Frossard's 145th Sale (April 20-21, 1897), Lot 375 mentioned a combination of his Monograph obverse 7 with reverse of his No. 8, which would be a union of obverse 9 with reverse I (shown on my plate II). This combination is known by this example only. The piece was secured by Dr. Thomas Hall, of Boston, but unfortunately was received too late to refer to it except in this manner.

of the other leaf, joins a slender horizontal branch below; this branch reaches from above the top of 7 to that of 3. The R is over the hair close above the forehead, and the date about midway between the hair and the point of the bust. A light line may be seen upon most specimens, extending from the point of the bust toward the border. I find some in which it is scarcely visible, whereas others show it as a slight crack. Mr. Frossard's No. 6 was from the same die with this, but the difference which he notes between his 6 and 7, it is now generally conceded, is due to a bruise on the sprig, turning aside the stem of the leaf on the left, and apparently joining it with that of the central leaf, thus producing the appearance of a different sprig.

Had I pursued my studies of this increasing crack with reference to the two reverses found with this obverse, before the pieces were arranged for engraving, I should have transposed reverses G and H, as I find the obverses showing this fault the least are coupled with reverse H, conclusively proving that to have been the one earliest in use. This is the die most commonly imitated in the Smith counterfeits, and is the one, when coupled with reverse H, most easily obtained; but with reverse G, it is much more difficult to find.

Reverse G, with obverse 9. $\frac{ONE}{CENT}$ high, the centre-mark below the middle of CENT. On the left branch are twelve ovate and three trefoil leaves, and on the right, fourteen ovate and two trefoil; the upper trefoil on the left is under the first T of STATES, the four others all on line with the top of the bow; the upper leaf on the left points between two on the right; the left branch has seven sprays of berries outside and four inside; the right, eight outside and one inside; the upper spray, of seven berries, springs from the stem back of the second leaf, is long, and points at s; the stems reach as far as the middle of the legend, ending at about one millimeter from it at the left, and about two at the right. The bow is heavy, high and triangular, nearly filling the space under CENT; the ribbon ends are heavy and of about equal length with the stems. The fraction central; the regula slightly curved, reaching nearly across the space; 100 widely spaced, the last cipher high. This die is usually found with a crack from the last A across the centre-mark to the first

T of STATES. This is the reverse more rarely found with obverse 9, and is the only one with three trefoils on one branch and only two on the other.

Reverse H, with obverse 9. ONE CENT nearly central, the centre-mark very light, on top of N. The left branch bears eleven ovate and two trefoil leaves; the right, twelve ovate and two trefoil; all the trefoils are on line with CENT: the upper leaf of the right branch points at the side of that at the left: the sprays are five and three at the left, five and four at the right; a spray of four (?) berries, starts from the tip of the upper leaf, and points midway between s and o. The stem at the left joins the ribbon for about half its length, that at the right is longer than the ribbon end and quite near its upper half. The bow is large, less angular than in G, and highest at the right. The fraction is low, central; the regula straight and heavy, resting on the denominator, which is closely spaced, and joins the ribbon ends by a fine line or a crack. It is usually found with cracks across CA and the ribbon ends, from R to the lower leaves on the right, and sometimes a light crack through UNITED.

Obverse 10, with reverses F and I. The head is much like that of obverse 8, the locks of hair cleanly cut, but the lower three more equally separated and more divergent, the lowest nearly reaching the border; the double curl does not join the sprig, the stem of which has a heavy end, as if retaining a small piece broken from the branch, and rises close over the space between 7 and 9; the leaves are narrow, the two outer at a right angle with each other, the centre leaf leaning slightly to the right, the sprig erect and near the hair. The letters of the legend are much like those of obverse 8, but more widely spaced and nearer the head; T is over the forehead close to the hair. The date is like that of obverse 9, but more widely spaced, and is nearer the hair than to the point of the bust.

This die I consider quite rare, and, coupled with reverse F, is so far as I know, unique.

Reverse I, with obverse 10. ONE CENT nearly central, the centre-mark scarcely visible on top of N. Twelve ovate and two trefoil leaves on the left branch, eleven ovate and two trefoil upon the right; the trefoils are all nearly on line with CENT: the points of two upper leaves nearly meet; seven sprays of berries outside and three inside the left branch, five outside and four inside the right; the upper spray, of three berries, starts from the side of the upper leaf and points at o. The left stem is short and joins the tip end of the ribbon near o, the right hand stem is long, reaching to the outer circle of the legend, at about two millimeters from its end, and the ribbon end near it is fully as long. The bow is medium size, similar in form to that of reverse H, and widest at the left. The legend is followed by a period; this occurs, in this class, only in reverses I and J. The fraction is high, to the left; the regula straight, joining the ribbon at the left, and nearer the first two figures of the denominator; the space between 1 and 00 wide. [See note 2 on p. 25.]

Obverse 11, with reverse J. The head resembles Nos. 9 and 10, but the middle locks of hair are shorter and the third long lock double at its end; the double curl nearly joins the upright leaf of the sprig. The left leaf of the sprig rises upright from close above the 9, the two others inclining to the right, the lower leaf extending horizontally over and beyond the 3. The legend and date are much like those of No. 10, but the date is farther from the border and within one millimeter of the hair, and four from the point of the bust. The letter R is placed as in obverses 5, 6 and 9.

Reverse J, with obverse 11. ONE CENT nearly central, the centre-mark on top of N. Twelve ovate and two trefoil leaves on the left branch (which is not joined between the two trefoils), and thirteen ovate and two trefoil upon the right; the trefoils on the left are between 1 and C; those on the right on line with CENT; five sprays of berries outside and three inside each branch; the upper spray is long, nearly stemless, starting between the two end leaves, and points between o and s; the upper end leaf on the right points between two at the left; the stems are about equal in length, reaching as far as the middle of the legend, terminating at about equal distances from each end. The bow is of medium size and but little curved at top or sides; the left end of the ribbon is shorter, and less deeply forked than that on the right, which is sharply curved near the knot joining the stem. The fraction is to the right; the regula very light, curved and close to the ribbon end at the right; the numerator is high above the regula, and the denominator nearly as much below it. The legend is followed by a period, as in I, but is here at the end of a spray of berries, and it has been doubted whether it was intended for a period or for a berry. Many of the sprays of vines are without stems.

This Cent is most frequently found with edge lettered ONE HUNDRED FOR A DOLLAR — the letters on different pieces differing in size and direction of reading, but sometimes with vine and bars as on most of this class; occasionally one of either of the Cents of this year may be found with edges plain; though this, I think, is unintentional. With the lettered edge this is nearly as common as 9–H, but with vine and bars it is much more scarce.

CLASS 3. THE LIBERTY CAP CENTS.

The Cents of this class, which includes obverses 12, 13 and 14, with reverses K and L, derive their name from the cap of Liberty which is here retained upon the staff, in still closer imitation than in Class 2, of the design of the French model, though differing in its treatment. The hair is shorter, flowing less freely, confined by a band or fillet passing over the top of the head but partly concealed by the hair, which is smooth, and as it falls in heavy locks behind the neck, shows the form of the head as in no other variety. The staff, supporting the Liberty cap, passes behind the neck over the left shoulder. These dies though bearing heads nearly identical, may be readily distinguished by the positions of the letters, and by the cracks upon two of them. I have no knowledge of an impression of either No. 13 or 14, from the die in its perfect condition.

The reverses have the words $\frac{ONE}{CENT}$ within a wreath formed by two olive branches, the fruit of which is borne singly on axillary stems; the stems of the branches below the knot, where they cross, are straight and slender, and are tied with a ribbon which forms a double bow within the wreath. The ribbon ends are long, falling below the stems, and in the space between them is the fraction $\frac{1}{100}$. The legend UNITED STATES OF AMERICA nearly encircles the wreath, and a circle of beads forms the border. They are struck on planchets of from 27 to 30 millimeters in diameter, and have edges lettered

ONE HUNDRED FOR A DOLLAR ✦ in letters varying in size and in the direction of the reading. This design was continued upon the Cents of 1794, 1795 and part of those of 1796.

Obverse 12, with reverses K and L. On this die one millimeter of the staff shows between the cap and the head. The first lock of hair under the cap is faint and indistinct, the lower lock ends in a sharp, hook-like curve, and the lock next above it is short and heavy. The lower end of the staff is in high relief, broad and rounded at its end, tapering toward the throat, less than its own diameter from the bust, and points nearly at one of the beads of the border. The cap, the date, and the first two letters of the legend are very close to the border; the other letters more distant from it. The border contains ninety-five beads. This is the most common die of this class.

Obverse 13, with reverse L. This is known as the "cracked die," a crack extending through the E, across the head and neck, passing close to right of 3. The hair is much like that of No. 12. About half a millimeter of the staff shows between the cap and the head, its lower end faintly cut, more than its own diameter from the bust, tapering but little toward the throat, and so faint at its end as to render it difficult to define its exact termination. The cap, the date, and the legend, are more distant from the border than in obverse 12, and more regular in that distance. I and R are high, E low, and TY more closely spaced than in that die. The border contains ninety-five beads. This die is much rarer than the preceding.

Obverse 14, with reverses K and L. This very rare die is also cracked, but not as conspicuously as is No. 13; the crack is faintly seen from a bead of the border, across the right top of Y to the forehead, and again from the lower lock of hair to the border. The lower lock ends in a heavier, hook-like curl, and those above it are more sharply pointed. About one-half millimeter of the staff shows behind the head, as in No. 13, but the lower end is in higher relief, more tapering toward the throat, nearly as far from the bust as in that, and points directly at a bead of the border, which contains ninety-seven beads. A minute point of difference in these dies may be found in the relative position of the letter I and the beads above it: in No. 12, two beads are directly over it (ı); in ı3, one is more nearly central above, and one over the left part of it (ı̄), and in ı4, one is central above it (ı). This is the rarest die of this class, and I can recall but two impressions from it.

Reverse K, with obverses ı2 and ı4. The left branch has fourteen leaves, eight in pairs and six single, with five olives, one of which is just at the left of the bow; the right branch has sixteen leaves, fourteen in pairs and two single, and seven olives; the lower two leaves at the left of the knot are broad and single, and the upper leaf of the left branch points between two of the right; one leaf on the right comes very close to the right foot of the letter м. The stem at the left passes in front of the ribbon end, and points just to the right of υ; that at the right passes from the knot nearly parallel with, and close to the ribbon, forming a narrow loop, then behind it, pointing at the right foot of ʌ. Both of the ribbon ends pass through the knot, the left end not falling below the regula, the right end falling to the middle of the ciphers, and more sharply pointed. The regula rests upon the figure ı, and the border is of eighty-five beads.

Reverse L, with obverses ı2, ı3 and ı4. The left branch has fourteen leaves, ten in pairs and four single, with six olives, two of which are nearly under the bow; the olives upon this branch are mostly smaller than those on the right, but the upper one is larger; the right branch has eighteen leaves, twelve in pairs, three single, and near the top a group of three, with five olives; the two lower leaves at each side of the knot are narrow and in pairs, and the points of two upper terminal leaves nearly meet; the stems cross the ribbon ends as in reverse K, but that at the right is longer, reaching to the inner circle of the legend, and pointing close to the left of ʌ. The ribbon end at the right does not pass through the knot, but leaves the bow well above it, passing in front of the branch and stem, forming with them a small triangle between itself and the knot, and falls just across the regula; the ribbon end at the left falls lower, reaching as far as the middle of the denominator, and well to the left of it. ı is high nearly joining the regula, and the border has ninety-one beads. This die is common, as compared with the other reverse.

For the convenience of those who may not be familiar with the Smith counterfeits of these Cents, I give upon Plate III illustrations of several of them. The heads are all in low relief, the outlines when examined with a glass appear ragged, and the field rough, as though eaten out by acid, as they probably were. Those oftenest seen are copied from No. 9–G but not so closely that they may not be easily detected by comparison with the plates.

THE following table of equivalents may be convenient for those who are familiar with previous tables of these Cents. The larger number given by Doughty does not indicate so many different obverse dies, as he gives a new number to every combination, and I find no difference in the dies given by him as 5 and 6, though every known Cotton Leaf Cent has been submitted for examination, and all three of them were in my hands at the same time and were very carefully compared. Numbers 2 and 8 were unknown when the previous tables were issued.

CROSBY 1897.	LEVICK 1869.	FROSSARD 1878.	DOUGHTY 1890.	CROSBY 1897.	LEVICK 1869.	FROSSARD 1878.	DOUGHTY 1890.
1	1	1	1 & 2	8	—	—	—
2	—	—	—	9	7	6 & 7	10 & 11
3	2	3	3	10	8	8	9
4	3	2	4	11	9	9	12
5	6	10	5 & 6	12	10	11	13 & 14
6	4	4	7	13	11	12	15
7	5	5	8	14	12	13	16 & 17

PLATE III.
THE CENTS AND HALF-CENTS OF 1793.
With the Smith Counterfeits.

THE HALF CENTS OF 1793.

UCH less interest has been taken in the collection of the different dies of Half Cents of this year than of the Cents, and it is difficult to find a cabinet containing many of them. I can add no new dies in the regular series to those already described by Mr. E. Frossard in his "Monograph," but can only describe those dies more minutely.

Before attempting this I will introduce a piece referred to by Mr. W. S. Baker, in his "Medallic Portraits of Washington," as follows: "The portrait . . . struck with a reverse of the Half Cent of 1793 — the first year of the regular coinage, — is different again from all others in this list, and may have been copied from the original by Edward Savage, painted in New York in 1790. The transposition from three-quarter face into a profile will account for the difference in expression. The head is in quite high relief, altogether unsuited for a coin, and the piece may be considered in the light of a fancy production not intended as a pattern."

The piece here referred to bears upon its obverse a military bust of Washington facing the right, with the legend LIBERTY above, and the date 1793 in exergue (Plate III). The legend and the date, excepting the figure 3, which has a rounded top instead of the straight horizontal line, as in the regular coinage, agree closely with those of obverse 2 of the Half Cents. The reverse is the same as reverse A, and the edge is lettered as on those.

It is impossible to state with certainty that this was intended as a pattern, but as it has every appearance of a genuinely struck piece, with reverse from a die used with the Half Cents of the regular issue, I am inclined to believe it to have been so intended, and therefore give it a place upon the plate as a pattern. As to the objection of its high relief, the same might with nearly as much reason be urged against most of the coins of this year.

Of these coins I have found but two obverse and three reverse dies. Frossard mentions four reverse dies, but from a close examination of his plate, comparing his 1 and 4 with each other and with original impressions, I can detect no difference in them except that noted by him in the "dividing line of the fraction," which he describes as "short, thick, and touches the upper curve of the 2, while distant from the last cipher." I find no impression showing the peculiarity of his No. 4, but the die agrees so perfectly in all other respects with reverse A and with No. 1 of his plate that I think it must be the same die, altered in that line, either in the die or upon the coin itself.

The design of the obverses is similar to that of the Liberty Cap Cents, but with the head facing left. The fillet band is visible entirely across the head, from just above the forehead to near the staff behind. The edges are lettered TWO HUNDRED FOR A DOLLAR ~ ~

Obverse 1 with reverses A and B. The letter L is partly over the hair and low, the Y not more than half a millimeter from the cap, and TY high. The cap has a rounded top, is narrow at its base, the right hand outline having but two curves, making it narrow in the middle. The upper lock of hair extends fully under and slightly beyond the cap, nearly parallel with its lower line; the second, third and fourth are longer, and the lowest ends in a curl underneath. The end of the staff lays very close to the line of the bust. The date is widely spaced, the 1 high and the 7 small.

Obverse 2 with reverses A and B. The letters L and TY low; L is entirely over the forehead, and the V fully one millimeter from the cap, which is more pointed at the top and more broad at the base than in obverse 1, having three curves on its right hand outline, and being full in the middle. The upper lock of hair is short, pointing nearly at the middle of the base of the cap, the second reaches nearly to the outer edge of the cap, the third is much longer, pointing downward, and the fourth appears to turn under with the lowest, which forms a curl underneath,— though in some impressions a faint outline of a point to it may be detected. The end of the staff is more than twice its own diameter from the line of the bust. The date is closely spaced, the 7 large and the 9 and 3 high.

These pieces are usually designated in sale catalogues as the small, or the large 7.

The reverses closely resemble those of the Cents of Class 2, but the branches are without trefoil leaves, these bearing only ovate leaves and racemes of small berries, and have the words HALF CENT within the wreath. The larger number of sprays are on the outside of the branches.

Reverse A with obverses 1 and 2. One millimeter space between HALF and CENT, the centre-mark large, and nearer the right foot of A. Each branch bears fifteen leaves, the points of the two upper terminal leaves nearly meeting under s. The stems cross, forming nearly a right angle under the knot, that at the left very near the U, that at the right joining the ceriph of the foot of A. The sprays of berries on the left are five and three; on the right, five and four. The top of the bow is nearly straight, the ribbon ends rather heavy and forked, that at the left most deeply, that at the right longer, reaching nearly (or quite?) to the border. The regula is curved, joining the ribbon end at the left, and close under the numerator. The figure 2 is high and very near the ribbon end. The legend is close around the wreath but more than one millimeter from the border.

Reverse B with obverse 2. One and one-half millimeters between HALF and CENT, the centre-mark small and near the left top of N. The left branch bears thirteen leaves, one inside joining H; the right, fourteen; the tips of two terminal leaves nearly meeting under E S. The stems are long, forming a wide angle, extending as far as the outer circle of the legend, and nearly equidistant from U and A. The sprays on the left are six and three; on the right seven and three. The top of the bow curves slightly downward. The ends of the ribbon are heavy, and forked half their length or more, the streamers from both nearly reaching the border. The regula is slightly curved and central, and the denominator widely spaced. The legend is about equally distant from wreath and border.

Reverse C with obverse 1. About one millimeter between HALF and CENT. No centre-mark, but a period follows CENT. A period also follows the legend. Fifteen leaves upon the left branch and sixteen upon the right. The upper terminal leaf on the right extends over that at the left, nearly meeting the point of the second leaf on that side under E. Six sprays outside and four inside each branch. The stems are slender, forming a wide angle, that at the left short, joining the U, that at the right much longer, reaching as far as the outer circle of the legend, and ending about two millimeters from A. The top of the bow is deeply curved in the centre and highest on the left. The ribbon ends are light, that at the right longest, and most deeply forked. The regula is long, straight and very light. The 2 is high; the first cipher low, and near the second. The legend is nearer the border on the right than on the left.

It is difficult to estimate the rarity of these coins, owing to the lack of interest in their collection; but I should judge the obverses to be about equal in that respect; reverse A the most common, and B and C very much more rare.

The descriptions I have given comprise every die of the U. S. Coins of 1793 at present known to collectors. Should any others be discovered I shall be glad to be informed, that descriptions, and if possible illustrations, may be given in a supplementary leaf.

www.ingramcontent.com/pod-product-compliance
Lightning Source LLC
Chambersburg PA
CBHW032140080426
42733CB00008B/1136